CORDELIA HARVEY

Other Badger Biographies

CORDELIA HARVEY
Civil War Angel

Bob Kann

WISCONSIN HISTORICAL SOCIETY PRESS

Published by the Wisconsin Historical Society Press
Publishers since 1855

© 2011 by the State Historical Society of Wisconsin

Publication of this book was made possible in part by a grant from the D.C. Everest fellowship fund.

wisconsin**history**.org

Photographs identified with WHi are from the Society's collections; address requests to reproduce these photos to the Visual Materials Archivist at Wisconsin Historical Society, 816 State Street, Madison, WI 53706.

Front cover: WHi Image ID 36009. Back cover: WHi Image ID 10805.

Printed in the United States of America
Cover and interior design by Jill Bremigan
Interior page composition by Biner Design

15 14 13 12 11   1 2 3 4 5

Library of Congress Cataloging-in-Publication Data
Kann, Bob.
  Cordelia Harvey : Civil War angel / Bob Kann.
      p. cm.—(Badger biographies)
  Includes bibliographical references and index.
  ISBN 978-0-87020-458-6 (pbk. : alk. paper) 1. Harvey, Cordelia A. P. (Cordelia Adelaide Perrine),
1824–1895—Juvenile literature. 2. United States—History—Civil War, 1861–1865—Women—
Juvenile literature. 3. United States—History—Civil War, 1861–1865—War work—Juvenile
literature. 4. United States—History—Civil War, 1861–1865—Hospital—Juvenile literature.
5. Governors' spouses—Wisconsin—Biography—Juvenile literature. 6. Women—Wisconsin—
Biography—Juvenile literature. 7. Wisconsin—History—Civil War, 1861–1865—Biography—
Juvenile literature. 8. United States—History—Civil War, 1861–1865—Biography—Juvenile
literature. 9. Soldiers—Services for—Wisconsin—History—19th century—Juvenile literature. 10.
Orphanages—Wisconsin—History—19th century—Juvenile literature. I. Title.
  E628.K36 2011
  973.7'77092—dc22
  [B]

                                        2010027443

This book is dedicated to Mary Gallagher, Lilian Eufracio, Dulce Coladilla, and Trinidad Navarro. Thank you for the loving care you provided for my mother, Ann.

Contents

1

Meet Cordelia

Imagine that you are a soldier in wartime. You are in the hospital because you are very sick or have been wounded in battle. The hospital is more than 500 miles from your home. None of your friends or family can visit you because the war is being fought near your hospital.

You are lying on a **cot** in the same room with hundreds of soldiers. Only one doctor is there to take care of everyone. Your only nurses are other sick patients who have no training to care for you.

You're feeling sad, lonely, and in pain. What might make you feel better? For many Wisconsin soldiers during the **Civil War**, it was **Cordelia** Harvey. Cordelia's job was to help the soldiers. She did her job so well that soldiers often asked for her to come to help take care of them when they were in the hospital.

cot: an army bed **Civil War**: the war between the North and South of the United States, which took place between 1861 and 1865 **Cordelia**: kor **deel** yuh

1

Cordelia would visit the soldiers, bring them tasty things to eat and drink, say kind words, read letters to them from home, and write letters for them. She convinced the army generals to change the hospital rules so that the sick soldiers received better care. Sometimes she even helped soldiers return home.

Because of her good work, many newspapers called Cordelia the "Wisconsin Angel." She did not like the name. She wrote, "I am simply doing my **duty** & doing very little compared with the great amount there is to be done."

Cordelia did much more than her duty, though. She convinced the president of the United States, Abraham Lincoln, to open a hospital for soldiers in Wisconsin. She also made sure that many children were taken care of after their fathers died in the Civil War. She saved thousands of lives and made many soldiers' final days easier. This is the story of how one Wisconsin woman made life better for soldiers and their families in what was perhaps the worst war in United States history.

duty: something someone is required to do

2

"She Could Run Like a Deer"

The Perrin family **coat of arms**. The family changed the spelling to Perrine after they moved to the United States.

On December 7, 1824, Cordelia **Perrine** was born in the town of **Barre** Center, New York. Cordelia was the daughter of John Perrine and Mary Hibbard. She had 5 younger sisters, an older stepsister, and an older stepbrother. The Perrines were related to the royal family of Henry IV of France, who ruled as the king of France from 1589 to 1610.

Perrine: pair **ruhn**   Barre: **bair** ee   **coat of arms**: a design in the shape of a shield that is used as the special sign of a family or city

WHI IMAGE ID 35754

A view of Southport from Lake Michigan in 1844.

In 1840, the Perrine family moved to **Kenosha**, Wisconsin, just south of Milwaukee. At the time it was known as Southport. John and Mary became successful farmers. Although she was only 16 years old, Cordelia became a schoolteacher at a school called the Southport Academy.

What was Cordelia like as a teacher? One of her students described her as sometimes behaving like a teenager and at other times acting like a grown-up: "At recess time she would

Kenosha: kuh **noh** shuh

take off her shoes and play **'pull-away'** with the crowd; she could run like a deer and be just like one of the big girls; but when school called and she got her shoes on again, she became at once the **schoolmistress** in full control."

Louis Harvey was the principal and a teacher at Southport Academy. Louis was born in East Haddam, Connecticut, on July 22, 1820. He attended college for 2 years and then became a teacher in Ohio and Kentucky. Louis moved to Kenosha, Wisconsin, in 1841, where he immediately began working at the Southport Academy.

WHI IMAGE ID 37904

Louis taught the older students, while Cordelia taught children younger than 10 years old. Both taught many subjects that are still taught today, including reading, writing, grammar, math, geography, and history.

This portrait of Louis Harvey, taken in 1860, captures his kindness.

pull-away: a game similar to tag   **schoolmistress**: a woman who teaches in a school

5

Until 1880, when the United States government began to pay for children to attend school, students had to pay to go to Southport Academy. Older students paid $3 ($225 in today's money) every 3 months, and younger students paid $2 ($150 in today's money).

In 1847, Cordelia and Louis were married. Afterward, they moved to Clinton Junction, 60 miles west of Southport. There, Louis opened a **general store**. Their daughter, Mary, was born in Clinton in 1848. Mary died 4 years later from "canker rash," which is now called **scarlet fever**. Cordelia would have no more children of her own, but her neighbors remembered "the love Cordelia showed for all children."

MINNESOTA

Lake Superior

Where the Harveys Lived

N

MICHIGAN

WISCONSIN

Mississippi River

Lake Michigan

IOWA

Madison ★

Milwaukee

Waterloo (Shopiere)

0   50 miles
0   50 kilometers

Turtle Creek

Clinton Junction (Clinton)

Southport (Kenosha)

AMELIA JANES, EARTH ILLUSTRATED, INC.

general store: a store that sells a variety of items such as clothing and tools   **scarlet fever**: a serious and quickly spreading illness that occurs mostly in children, and causes a bright red rash, a sore throat, and a high fever

A few years later in 1851, Louis and Cordelia moved to Waterloo, Wisconsin, where Louis opened a flour mill along Turtle Creek. He built the mill to grind the wheat grown in the community around the Turtle Creek dam. Louis and Cordelia lived in a two-story house in Waterloo. Louis **persuaded** his neighbors to change the name of their town from Waterloo to *Shopiere* from a French word meaning **limestone** because there was a lot of limestone in that area.

Louis Harvey started this flour mill in Shopiere in 1851.

persuaded: convinced someone to do something by giving the person good reasons   **Shopiere:** shoh **peer**
limestone: a hard rock used in building and in making cement

A blacksmith who knew Louis and Cordelia in Shopiere remembered that both were "serious folk." Louis, he said, was the **best-informed** man in the area since he regularly read 2 or 3 newspapers.

For years, Louis had been developing his leadership skills. Louis became active in Wisconsin **politics** shortly after the Harveys moved to Clinton Junction. In 1847, he was elected to the Wisconsin **Constitutional Convention**. This was the meeting where men wrote the Wisconsin Constitution, that is, the laws for the state of Wisconsin. Louis became known as one of the best speakers at the convention even though he was one of the youngest members. When Wisconsin became a state in 1848, Louis's name was known by many of the men who helped to create its laws.

In 1852, Louis was elected a **state senator** from Rock County. He served as a state senator until 1859, when he was elected **secretary of state** of Wisconsin. The Harveys

best-informed: having the most knowledge or information   politics: the way a city, county, state, or nation governs itself   constitutional (kon stuh **too** shuhn uhl) convention: a meeting where state leaders write down what rights and responsibilities people of the state will have and how the government will work   state senator: a member of the state senate, the group that determines the laws of the state   secretary of state: the person elected as keeper of the official records of the government of a particular state

then moved to Madison, the **capital** of Wisconsin. Two years later, Louis was elected **governor** of Wisconsin. The Civil War had just begun. The war changed the Harveys' lives in ways they never could have imagined, as it did for most Americans.

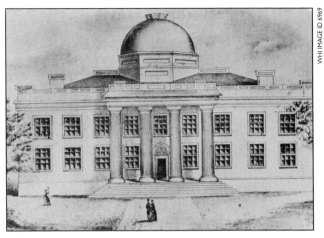

WHI IMAGE ID 6969

The second Wisconsin capitol building as it looked when Louis Harvey was a state senator.

capital: the city where the state government is located to represent all of the people of the state   **governor**: the person elected as the head of the state

Why Did the United States Fight the Civil War?

During the first half of the 1800s, people in the United States argued over the issue of slavery. Generally, people from Northern states were opposed to slavery, while people from Southern states supported it.

Geography explains some of the difference. Cotton was an important crop that could be easily grown in the South with its long growing season. Many cotton **plantations** relied on the work of African American slaves, who were not paid for their **labor**. Most slave owners believed they couldn't make money without the work of slaves. In the North, many people wanted slavery to be **abolished**. They believed slavery was wrong and that all people should be free to live and work as they wished. The differences between the North and the South created a great divide across the growing nation.

Abraham Lincoln was part of the new Republican Party, which was against slavery. When Lincoln was elected president in 1860, many people from the South worried that slavery would be abolished and their cotton plantations would fail. Many people in the South wanted to leave the **Union**.

geography (jee **og** ruh fee): the study of the earth, including its people, resources, climate, and physical features **plantation**: a large farm   **labor**: work   **abolished** (uh **bol** ishd): officially ended   **Union** (**yoo** nyuhn): the group of states that remained loyal to the United States government during the Civil War; the North

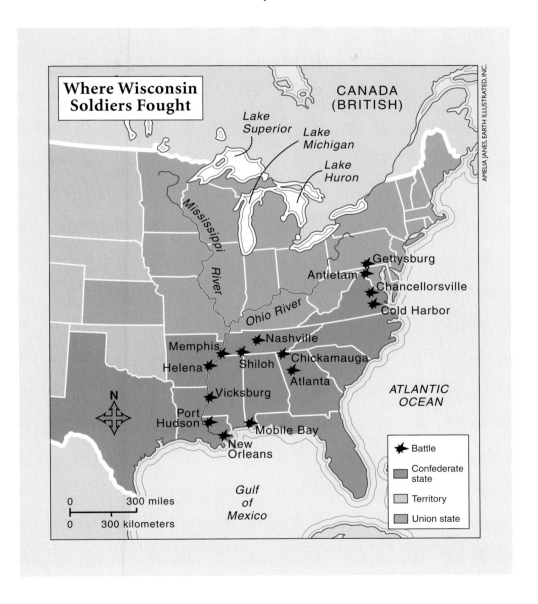

They wanted to form their own country where slavery would be legal. Before President Lincoln took office, 7 Southern states had already **seceded**—first, South Carolina, followed by Mississippi, Florida, Alabama, Georgia, Louisiana, and Texas. These states formed their own country, which they named the **Confederate States of America**.

On April 12, 1861, Confederate troops attacked Fort Sumter, a Union fort on the coast of South Carolina. Soon more states joined the Confederacy: **Arkansas**, North Carolina, Virginia, and **Tennessee**. Four more states decided to stay with the Union: **Missouri**, Kentucky, Maryland, and Delaware. That meant more states sided with the Union. But that didn't mean war would be over quickly.

---

seceded (si **see** ded): left or withdrew from a group or an organization, often to form another   **Confederate** (kuhn **fed** ur it): related to the group of 11 Southern states who fought the Northern states during the Civil War
Arkansas: ahr kin saw   **Tennessee:** ten uh **see**   **Missouri:** muh **zur** ee

3

The Soldier's Friend

When Louis Harvey became governor of Wisconsin in
January 1862, the Civil War had been going on for about
9 months. Many men from Wisconsin had volunteered to
fight for the Union. Madison had the largest training area
for soldiers in Wisconsin at Camp Randall. There, 70,000
men trained for war. Today, Camp Randall is the site of the
University of Wisconsin's football stadium. Soldiers in
training learned to follow orders and to march with rifles.
These **drills**, which they practiced over and over, taught them
the **discipline** they needed on the **battlefield**.

From the start, Governor Harvey was well liked by the
people of Wisconsin. The governor quickly developed a
reputation as being a friend of Wisconsin soldiers. As the
new governor, one of the first things he did was to ask the

drill: learning through repeating the same action over and over   **discipline** (**dis** uh plin): control over the way
you act or behave   **battlefield**: an area where a battle is being fought   **reputation** (rep yoo **tay** shuhn): the
opinion that people have about someone or something

Soldiers drilling at
Camp Randall.

WHI IMAGE ID 1838

WHI IMAGE ID 4225

Camp Randall
soldiers sharpen
their skills for battle.

state **legislature** to provide more money for soldiers on the
battlefield and for their families at home. He also visited
soldiers near the battlefield to cheer them up and see that
they had the food and care they needed.

legislature (**lej** uh slay chur): a group of people elected by citizens who have the power to make the laws for
the state

The soldiers liked Governor Harvey, too. A **company** of volunteers even named themselves after the governor. They were called the "Harvey **Zouaves**." When the Harvey Zouaves left Wisconsin to fight, Cordelia gave each soldier a Bible.

WHI IMAGE ID 11296

THE MADISON ZOUAVES
FOR
THE WAR!

This Co. which has been organized and in active Drill

FOR MORE THAN A YEAR, HAS ENLISTED FOR THE WAR!

Under the recent call by the President of the United States. For the purpose of filling the ranks to the required number, a commission has been specially issued by the Governor to the undersigned, the Captain of the Company. The

ARMORY OF THE COMPANY, IN THE CITY HALL AT MADISON,
IS NOW OPENED AS THE RECRUITING OFFICE.

All the advantages of enlisting in connection with a *well drilled Company*, and of enlisting for a new regiment, are here presented together. The

HIGHEST BOUNTY & PAY!

given to volunteers, will be given to the men of this Company. The undersigned was a member of the Old Governor's Guard from its earliest orgnaization until called, in 1861, to command the Madison Zouaves; and can satisfy any applicant as to his competency as a military officer.

The ranks of the Company will be filled by volunteer enlistments by the 15th of August, or after that date 🖙DRAFTING WILL BEGIN!🖙

The Drafted Soldier gets $11 a month only,& no Bounty!
The Volunteer gets the full Pay and all Bounties!!

🖙The pay of Volunteers will begin from the time of enlistment at full rates. What able-bodied man will desert his country in her hour of peril? Where is the coward who will shrink from the contest for the maintenance of our institutions and the preservation of our Constitution! Where the poltroon who will see our flag trampled by rebels and traitors, without a blow!! Rally Men of Dane County! Fill the ranks of our armies with brave hearts and strong hands! for the rescue of the Union!!

[Wisconsin State Journal Print, Madison.] **WM. F. VILAS, Recruiting Officer.**

How much money per month would a soldier make by volunteering?

company: a unit of 50 to 100 soldiers   Zouave (zoo ahv or zwahv): the name of several volunteer regiments in the Civil War

Women in the Civil War

When the Civil War began, many women were **frustrated**. They couldn't join the army because only men were allowed to fight. They couldn't give their opinions by voting since only men were allowed to vote. But they still wanted to help in the war effort.

The First Battle of Bull Run was the first major battle of the Civil War. It was fought on July 21, 1861, near **Manassas**, Virginia. People in the North hoped Union soldiers would win the battle and end the war. But it was not to be. Instead, Thomas "Stonewall" Jackson led Southern troops to victory. The cost of the battle was very high. Both sides were saddened by the violence and killing on the battlefield. People in Wisconsin and elsewhere realized the war would not be over soon. Instead, it would take many years, and many lives would be lost.

WHI IMAGE ID 7158I

Women prepare supplies to send to soldiers at a Soldiers' Aid Society office.

frustrated: feeling helpless and discouraged   **Manassas**: muh **na** sus

Immediately after Bull Run, Soldiers' **Aid Societies** were formed throughout Wisconsin. The women who belonged to these societies began by making bandages from **lint** and preparing other supplies for hospitals. Before long, the women started to make clothing and bed supplies such as pillows. The societies also collected money to supply soldiers with sewing kits, writing paper, and stamped envelopes. They helped the families of soldiers who had gone to war, too.

Cordelia served as the president of the Madison Ladies Aid Society.

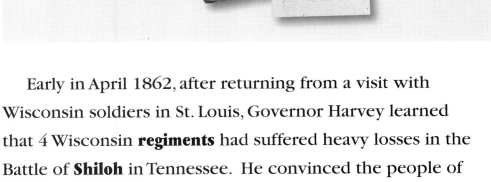

Soldiers used writing kits like this one to write letters home.

WISCONSIN VETERANS MUSEUM 98-1-392

Early in April 1862, after returning from a visit with Wisconsin soldiers in St. Louis, Governor Harvey learned that 4 Wisconsin **regiments** had suffered heavy losses in the Battle of **Shiloh** in Tennessee. He convinced the people of Wisconsin to collect medical supplies for the wounded

aid society (suh **sɪ** uh tee): a group that is formed to help others   **lint**: small bits of thread or fluff used like a bandage for covering wounds   **regiment** (**rej** uh muhnt): a unit of 500 to 1,000 soldiers   **Shiloh**: **shɪ** loh

soldiers. He personally delivered the supplies to the **army camps** and hospitals in Tennessee. Governor Harvey also persuaded several doctors to go with him on this trip.

On April 10, the governor and the doctors left Madison on a train to deliver the supplies. A Madison newspaper reported, "Everybody was eager to have those boxes get there safely, because they know how much they would mean to the boys, so Gov. Louis P. Harvey went down with them himself, saw that they were delivered, and talked to and encouraged the men."

On the way to Tennessee, the governor visited Wisconsin soldiers who were stationed in **Cairo, Illinois**; Mound City, Illinois; and **Paducah**, Kentucky. He cheered them up with kind words and showed them that their governor cared about them. On April 17, Governor Harvey arrived in Savannah, Tennessee, about 7 miles from where the Battle of Shiloh was fought. He was glad that he had made the trip. He wrote a letter to Cordelia saying, "Thank God for the **impulse** which brought me here. I am doing a good work."

army camp: a place where an army stays in tents or other temporary homes   Cairo, Illinois: **kair** oh il uh **noi**
Peducah: puh **doo** kuh   impulse: a sudden thought or idea that leads someone to take action or do something

Two days later, Governor Harvey prepared to return to Madison by boat. Late that rainy night as he was about to cross from one boat to another, his foot slipped. He fell into the Tennessee River. Governor Harvey drowned before he could be rescued.

WISCONSIN HISTORICAL MUSEUM 1969.4

Governor Harvey's pocketknife was found on his body. It had his initials, LPH, engraved on the blade.

WHI IMAGE ID 75528

Union steamboats docked at Pittsburg Landing on the Tennessee River, where Governor Harvey drowned.

After Governor Harvey drowned, a **telegram** was sent to Madison reporting the sad news to the head of Wisconsin's army, **Adjutant-General** Augustus Gaylord. General Gaylord was a good friend of Governor Harvey. Cordelia was in the State Capitol raising money to help soldiers' families when General Gaylord heard the news. He soon found **Nathaniel** Sawyer, Cordelia's brother-in-law, who worked at the Capitol. General Gaylord wanted Sawyer to help him take care of Cordelia when she learned of her husband's death.

They found Cordelia and asked her to come with them.

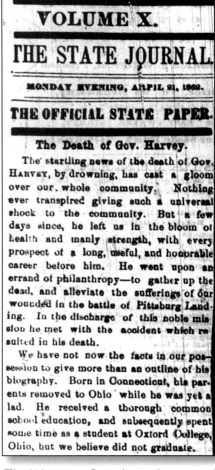

The *Wisconsin State Journal* reported on Governor Harvey's death.

---

telegram: a message that is sent by telegraph   adjutant-general (aj uh tuhnt   jen ruhl): the highest-ranking officer in the army after the governor   **Nathaniel**: nuh **than** yuhl

They had not told her what had happened. But Cordelia could tell from the looks on their faces that they were delivering bad news. She stopped them while they were walking and demanded, "Tell me if he is dead!" Before General Gaylord could answer, Cordelia fainted. When she awoke, she was taken home.

When news of the governor's death reached Madison, many people cried. Louis Harvey was only 42 years old and had been governor for only 94 days. Wisconsin had lost a good leader. The soldiers had lost a good friend. Cordelia had lost her husband.

4

"Can't I Go Home, Mrs. Harvey?"

After the funeral for Governor Harvey at the State Capitol, Cordelia returned to her house in Shopiere. Edward **Salomon**, the **lieutenant governor**, was sworn in as the new Wisconsin governor.

During the summer after Louis died, Cordelia grew sadder and sadder. She missed her husband and didn't know what to do next. She thought about becoming a teacher again but worried that she was too sad to teach young children well.

In August, Cordelia visited with Wisconsin Senator Timothy Howe. He suggested that she become Wisconsin's **allotment commissioner**. The job of an allotment commissioner was to visit the different companies of soldiers to decide how much of the soldier's **wages** should be sent home to his family. Soldiers were supposed to be paid every 2 months. But often,

Saloman: sah luh muhn   **lieutenant** (loo **ten** uhnt) **governor**: the second in command to the governor
allotment commissioner (kuh **mish** uh nur): person whose job it was to decide how much of soldiers' pay should be sent to their families   **wages**: the money someone is paid for his or her work

they didn't get paid until 4 or 6 months had gone by. When soldiers received their wages, the allotment commissioner made sure that soldiers sent enough money to provide for their families. The soldier's wages might be the only **income** that the family had.

Cordelia liked the idea of becoming an allotment commissioner. She realized that she could continue helping soldiers just as she had done with the Ladies Aid Society. And she would be visiting and working with soldiers just as Louis had done in his final days. Senator Howe thought that Cordelia would be very good at this job. He wrote, "It is the kind of labor to which she is fully **equal** and in which she would be, I am confident, very successful.... I know no one more energetic than she is in whatever interests her."

Senator Timothy Howe encouraged Cordelia to play a role in helping soldiers.

income: the amount of money someone earns or receives regularly   **equal**: able to handle

Women at Work in the Civil War

The Civil War created many new opportunities for women to work outside their homes. Thousands of young men had left home to become soldiers. This meant that women were now needed to do some of the jobs that had been done by men. Many women became nurses to help care for soldiers. Others took over farm work when their husbands left to fight. Some women worked as salespersons in the family store. Other women worked in offices or as government workers.

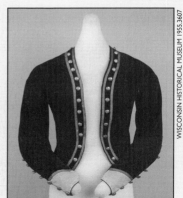

WISCONSIN HISTORICAL MUSEUM 1955.3607

This Union nurse's jacket was blue with gold buttons.

For a few women, the Civil War was a great opportunity. One woman named Mary Walker became a doctor. In 1863, she was the very first woman to be named an official army **surgeon**.

Here's something even more interesting. Did you know that more than 400 women actually fought in the Civil War? Of course, they had to disguise themselves as men. By law, women were not supposed to become soldiers. But women from both the North and the South believed in their cause so strongly that they were willing to pretend to be men so that they could fight.

surgeon (**sur** juhn): a doctor who performs surgery

When Governor Salomon heard that Cordelia wanted to help Wisconsin's soldiers, he had a different job in mind for her than being allotment commissioner. On September 10, 1862, he named Cordelia as Wisconsin's **sanitary** agent. Her job would be to make sure that the sick and wounded Wisconsin soldiers lying in hospitals

WHI IMAGE ID 34242

Cordelia reported directly to Governor Salomon.

along the Mississippi were being treated well. She would write reports to Governor Salomon telling him whether the sick and wounded Wisconsin soldiers were well cared for. She also would make suggestions to improve the care they received. Cordelia had no idea that this job would make her famous.

Two weeks after Cordelia became Wisconsin's sanitary agent, she arrived in St. Louis, Missouri. She rented a room in a hotel and began her job. On her first day, she visited 3 hospitals. She saw many Wisconsin soldiers in the hospitals

sanitary (**sa** nuh tair ree): having to do with being clean and healthy

25

receiving good care. She also saw many "Union ladies" who were helping the soldiers. The Union ladies were women who had traveled from their homes in the North to work in hospitals in the South where Union soldiers were **recovering**. According to Cordelia, these women worked hard and had "their whole heart in their work." Their help was clearly needed and welcomed.

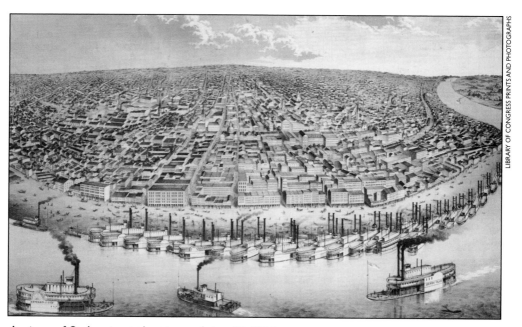

A view of St. Louis at the time of the Civil War.

recovering: getting better after illness or injury

A Civil War Nurse's Diary

Cordelia was one of hundreds of women from Wisconsin who traveled to hospitals along the Mississippi to help care for Wisconsin soldiers. Emilie Quiner, a young woman from Madison, was another. She spent 3 months in Memphis, Tennessee, during the summer of 1863. Here are 3 diary entries that Emilie wrote about her experience as a Civil War nurse.

Wednesday, July 8

The surgeon in charge, Dr. Hartshorn, came in and assigned us our **wards**. . . . The wards are long rooms containing from fifty to seventy beds. Each one has a surgeon, a **ward master** and four nurses besides a female nurse. There are some very sick men in my ward and being an entirely new business to me I went at it rather **awkwardly**. I expect that I shall soon learn how to work.

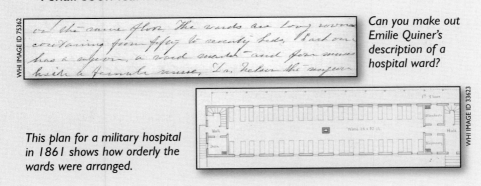

WHI IMAGE ID 75362

Can you make out Emilie Quiner's description of a hospital ward?

WHI IMAGE ID 33623

This plan for a military hospital in 1861 shows how orderly the wards were arranged.

ward: a large room or section in a hospital where patients are taken care of   **ward master**: the person in charge of a hospital ward   **awkwardly**: clumsily, without skill

Sunday, August 9

Today passed as usual. I was in my ward most of the time. James Farrell, a Wisconsin boy, had his finger **amputated** the other day, and his hand is very much swelled and **inflamed**. They brought him back to the ward today and he is very sick. I got him something nice to eat, bathed his head, and have sat by him most of the day. He suffers a great deal.

This is the kit a surgeon would carry.

WISCONSIN VETERANS MUSEUM 98-1-655

Tuesday, August 25

I packed my trunks and dressed myself after dinner and then went to **bid** the boys good bye. Poor boys, some of them cried at parting with me. I have been up there a good deal and it seemed very hard to go away and leave them so sick. I felt as bad at leaving my boys that it took away all the pleasure I had felt in the **prospect** of going home. Some seemed to feel sad at the thought that I was going to leave them. Poor fellows, they are so grateful for any kindness shown them. I shall miss my ward, and my poor sick boys, whether they do me or not.

amputated: cut off a part of the body because of disease or injury   **inflamed**: swollen   **bid**: tell or say
prospect: something that is looked forward to

After seeing what life was like for Union soldiers at the hospitals, Cordelia felt that she would also be able to make a difference. The soldiers were happy that she had been sent by Governor Salomon to look after their needs. They told her they were glad to be remembered by the governor.

Not everything about the job was easy for Cordelia. She had a difficult visit with a soldier from Oshkosh, Wisconsin. He was so weak that Cordelia thought he would soon die. He wanted to be home. As Cordelia reported in a letter to the governor, "The tears rolled down his cheeks when he spoke of home, & he said [it was] 'too late to do any thing now.' "

Cordelia visited hospitals at St. Louis, Cape **Girardeau**, Ironton, and Cairo.

Girardeau: juh **rahr** doh

29

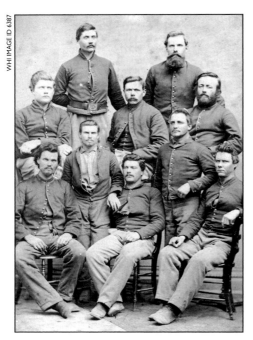

WHI IMAGE ID 6387

Some of these men fom the 1st Wisconsin Cavalry may have been among Cordelia's patients.

Cordelia was pleased to see that the St. Louis hospitals were well run. Next, she took a boat to Cape Girardeau, Missouri, 120 miles south on the Mississippi River. She had been told there were many Wisconsin soldiers in the hospitals there, too. Cordelia was shocked by what she saw in the first hospital she visited. She saw much pain and suffering. The hospital itself was dirty and overcrowded. The air was stuffy and smelled terrible. She found more than 150 men from the 1st Wisconsin **Cavalry** who were not doing well. She wrote to the governor that they looked "like ghosts of their former selves."

These men were sick and dying from many different diseases. The only nurses were other sick soldiers helping

cavalry (**ka** vuhl ree): soldiers who fight on horseback

Worse Than Bullets

Most Civil War soldiers believed that the bullet was their biggest enemy. In fact, disease was the biggest killer during the Civil War. Of the soldiers that died, 2 out of 3 died from **contagious** diseases like **dysentery** and **tuberculosis**.

Why did so many soldiers become ill? One reason was that young boys, old men, and others who were in poor health were allowed to join the army. Many young men got sick as soon as they joined the army because they had never been **exposed** to diseases like measles or chickenpox.

Diseases also spread quickly in the army camps because the camps were so dirty. Unclean water and food that was not fresh also spread deadly germs.

Today, we know a lot more about how disease is spread and what we can do to stop it. But in the Civil War, your neighbor's cough might be as deadly as your enemy's bullet.

as best they could, but some were too weak to be very useful. The hospital had only one doctor trying to take care of all these soldiers.

contagious: (kuhn **tay** jis): catching, able to be spread by close contact   **dysentery** (**dis** uhn tair ee): a contagious disease with symptoms of fever, diarrhea, and stomach pain   **tuberculosis** (tuh bur kyuh **loh** suhs): a highly contagious disease that affects the lungs, and often leads to death   **exposed**: put in contact with a contagious disease

Cordelia also visited a nearby military camp with the doctor. There, she saw more than 100 men lying on the grass or in tents waiting for help. She wrote home, "The sick men cry like children some of them are only boys, & say oh my Mother! My Mother! Can't I go home Mrs. Harvey?" One soldier was in so much pain that he told Cordelia he wished he were dead just like her husband.

Cordelia quickly learned how she could be helpful. She immediately began to look for new ways to improve the care of the soldiers. She learned what the soldiers needed to cheer them up. She brought them food and drinks. She decided to write to Governor Salomon to ask for more supplies, doctors, and nurses to help the soldiers.

WHI IMAGE ID 25729

Treating the wounded during a Civil War battle.

Cordelia worked very hard at her new job. She even apologized to the governor for the messy handwriting in her report about Wisconsin soldiers. She explained that she wrote the letter while talking to soldiers. She was so tired that her hand was shaking while she wrote. But at the same time, Cordelia felt herself becoming more confident as she saw how helpful she could be. She wrote to the governor, "I have passed through scenes that I trust will give me strength for future action. I am very well & am glad I came."

This is a list of supplies Cordelia ordered in 1862 for Wisconsin soldiers. Do any of the things on the list surprise you?

5

The Wisconsin Angel

Cordelia returned home to Madison after her trip to Cape Girardeau. She met with the governor to report what she saw and suggest what was needed in the hospitals. She also wanted women in Wisconsin to understand what more they could do to improve sick soldiers' lives. The *Wisconsin Daily State Journal* published Cordelia's letter to Wisconsin women telling them what they could do to help.

In this letter, Cordelia wanted to **inspire** women by telling them how much the soldiers appreciated the food they had sent. The soldiers would say, "Oh! Can't we have a little more, it is so good." Cordelia reminded the women that the soldiers were fighting to save their country. The women could help by sending food, clothing, blankets, towels, and medical supplies.

inspire: influence or encourage someone to do something

Cordelia soon returned to St. Louis and to the hospitals along the Mississippi River. She made many visits to every hospital in St. Louis during the next 6 months. Patients looked forward to her visits and knew they could receive help from her. She often wore a cape with a black hood. Soldiers spotted her easily. As Cordelia moved among the soldiers, she became known as the Wisconsin Angel. Soldiers would see her coming and beg her to help them.

Cordelia looked for even more ways to be useful to the soldiers. When she saw soldiers who she thought would never be healthy enough to fight again, she wrote the governor.

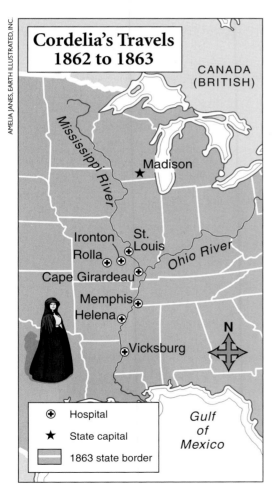

Cordelia's Travels 1862 to 1863

CANADA (BRITISH)

Mississippi River

★ Madison

Ironton
Rolla
St. Louis
Ohio River
Cape Girardeau
Memphis
Helena

Vicksburg

N

⊕ Hospital
★ State capital
▬ 1863 state border

Gulf of Mexico

AMELIA JANES, EARTH ILLUSTRATED, INC.

35

Why a Black Hood?

We don't know why Cordelia wore a black cape and hood when she took care of soldiers. But there are 2 likely reasons why she did.

Perhaps Cordelia wore the black hood because she was **mourning** the loss of her husband, Louis. Wearing dark clothing was one way people showed respect for the loss of a loved one in the 1800s. During the Civil War, women sometimes wore mourning clothes for as long as 2 years after their husbands died.

Cordelia also may have worn the black hood because it covered her head and hair. The hood made her less **attractive** to the soldiers that she was caring for. In 1861, Dorothy Dix was appointed **superintendent** of Union army nurses. This was the first organization of women to serve as nurses during the Civil War. Dix chose women she thought were "plain looking" and middle-aged. She thought that having pretty young nurses might lead to romances with the soldiers and cause many problems. Perhaps Cordelia wanted to avoid having such problems. By wearing a hood she could show that she was in mourning and also appear less attractive.

WHI IMAGE ID 36009

Cordelia was known for wearing a black hooded cape.

mourning (**mor** ning): feeling sadness or grief for someone who has died   **attractive**: pretty or handsome or pleasant to look at   **superintendent** (soo pur in **ten** dent): the person in charge of an organization

She suggested that they be **discharged** from the army and sent home. Before long, she began to try to convince the doctors in charge of the hospitals to send these soldiers home.

In November, Cordelia traveled to Ironton, Missouri, to visit soldiers from the 11th Wisconsin Regiment. She found more than 100 soldiers who were suffering from serious diseases like **typhoid**, **pneumonia**, and dysentery. They were all **unfit** for duty. They needed food and medical supplies. Cordelia made sure they received them.

Cordelia felt lucky to be treated so well by all of the soldiers and the doctors in the hospitals. She saw other people who were not treated so well. Women often were not welcomed in military hospitals. But Cordelia's actions were so helpful that she had no problems. She quickly earned the respect of the doctors and officers.

Cordelia was kind not only to Wisconsin soldiers or Union soldiers. She also cared about Confederate soldiers. In November, she visited Confederate prisoners in St. Louis.

---

discharged: officially told to leave the military   **typhoid** (**tɪ** foid): a contagious, often deadly disease with symptoms of high fever and diarrhea   **pneumonia** (nuh **mohn** yuh): a disease that causes the lungs to be filled with fluid, making breathing difficult   **unfit**: unable to serve because of illness or injury

She reported that many were very sick and needed to be sent north or they would soon die. She asked Governor Salomon to bring them to prison camps in Wisconsin to save their lives.

Less than 2 months after Cordelia began serving as Wisconsin's sanitary agent, the doctor in charge of the St. Louis hospital in Benton Barracks wrote a letter to Governor Salomon. The doctor praised Cordelia. He wrote that she had earned the respect of all the doctors in the hospital and the love and **gratitude** of the soldiers. She was gentle, kind, and friendly. If there was anything that could be done to help the soldiers, she did it. Nothing would stop her from helping them. He wished governors from other states had chosen sanitary agents as wisely as Governor Salomon had in his choice of Cordelia.

On November 17, Cordelia had a meeting with Major General Samuel Curtis. He gave her permission to visit all the hospitals under his command. This meant that she could go to any military hospital in Missouri, Arkansas, Illinois, and western Kentucky to help the sick and wounded from

gratitude: a feeling of being thankful

Wisconsin. He also gave an order to the **quartermasters** and transportation companies to give Cordelia all the supplies she needed and take her anywhere she wanted to go to do her work.

General Curtis praised Cordelia for her hard work.

Why did Major General Curtis do this for Cordelia? Perhaps because he had heard what good and important work she was doing and he wanted her to do even more of it. Or perhaps it was because 6 months earlier, his 20-year-old daughter had died from typhoid. Many soldiers died of typhoid and diseases like it. Maybe he hoped that Cordelia could save the lives of soldiers, many of whom were nearly the same age as his daughter.

In a hospital in Memphis, Tennessee, there were nearly 1500 patients. Cordelia stayed awake all night wondering if she could possibly visit all 1500 of them. Some of the men

quartermaster: an officer in charge of providing housing, clothing, food, fuel, and transportation for soldiers

Military Ranks

Ranks tell us the order of power in the military. The ranks may be different in different branches of the military, but in the army generals are at the top, and privates are at the bottom. From the top down, the order of military rank in the army is as follows:

1. General
2. **Colonel**
3. Lieutenant colonel
4. Major
5. Captain
6. Lieutenant
7. **Sergeant**
8. **Corporal**
9. Private

Navy Medal of Honor from the Civil War

The higher the rank, the more soldiers the officer commands. For example, a lieutenant is usually in charge of about 50 soldiers.

were from Wisconsin, but most were from other states. Cordelia realized that the only way she could help all of the sick and wounded Wisconsin soldiers would be to examine all 1500 soldiers in the hospital. She decided to do so.

Colonel: kur nuhl   **Sergeant: sahr** juhnt   **Corporal: cor** pur uhl

40

The next day, she went to see Colonel Allen, the **medical inspector** in charge of the hospital. He promised that if she made a list of the names of all the men she thought would never again be fit for service, he would send them home.

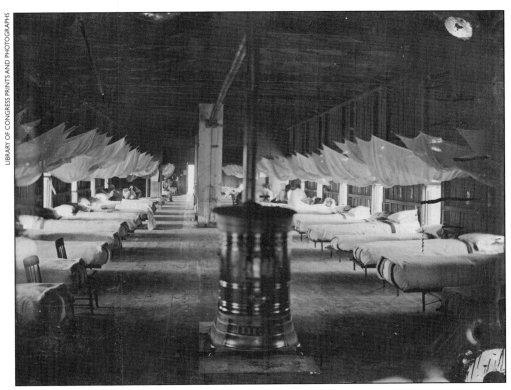

A typical Civil War hospital ward with beds lining the walls and mosquito netting that could be lowered to protect the patient.

medical inspector: the person who makes medical arrangements for a unit of the army

For 3 days, Cordelia worked from early morning until late at night. She visited all of the patients. She listed only the names of soldiers who she thought would never be well enough to fight again. Her list included the names of boys between the ages of 15 and 18, men over 60 years old, and soldiers who were wounded or had tuberculosis. When she finished the list, Colonel Allen kept his promise. He sent hundreds of Wisconsin soldiers home.

It was for actions like these that Cordelia was called "The Nightingale of Wisconsin" after another famous nurse, Florence Nightingale. People began to think of Cordelia as a hero. Cordelia did not like this. She was just doing her job. She wrote, "I do not wish to be 'Florence Nightingaled' nor any thing of the kind. I am simply doing my duty & doing very little compared with the great amount there is to be done."

Florence Nightingale
Leads the Way

The role that Cordelia played in taking care of soldiers during the Civil War was similar to what Florence Nightingale had done just a few years earlier. Florence Nightingale was born in 1820 into a wealthy family in England. Usually women from wealthy families would marry and become housewives. Instead, Florence Nightingale chose to care for sick and wounded soldiers.

Florence lived during a time period when nurses usually were poor women with little training in caring for their patients. Florence was different. She trained as a nurse in Germany. She was running a hospital for women in London when the **Crimean War** started.

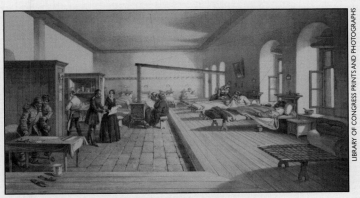

Florence Nightingale caring for patients in her ward.

Crimean (krɪ **mee** uhn) **War**: a war between Russia and Turkey, Great Britain, France, and Sardinia fought from 1853 to 1856

In 1854, she led a group of 38 English nurses to the Crimean **Peninsula** where they took care of the wounded.

Florence found the hospital conditions in Crimea to be terrible. Many of the wounded were unwashed. They were sleeping in overcrowded, dirty rooms without blankets or healthy food. Disease spread quickly in these conditions. Many soldiers died from infections and illnesses. Florence and her nurses worked to change these conditions. They set up a kitchen, fed the wounded from their own supplies, and cleaned the hospitals. They saved many lives with their care.

After the war, Florence returned to England. She became a hero because of the care she and the other nurses had provided the soldiers. Because of her example and her success, nursing became a respected job for women.

In 1859, Florence Nightingale published a book called *Notes on Nursing*. Many American women read it. They wanted to be nurses like Florence. When the Civil War started, Cordelia Harvey and many women like her took care of soldiers just as Florence Nightingale had done.

peninsula (puh **nin** suh luh): a piece of land that sticks out from another land mass and is almost completely surrounded by water

6

"Do Not Fear to Ask Me to Do Anything"

Cordelia admired the spirit of the sick and wounded Wisconsin soldiers. The sick soldiers often became weaker and weaker. They were surrounded by other soldiers who were in pain and suffering. Yet they were brave, cheerful, and didn't complain. Cordelia wrote that perhaps these sick soldiers showed more courage in the hospital than they had on the battlefield.

Cordelia was particularly saddened by the young boys she met on her rounds. She wrote about a soldier 16 years old whose "sufferings were more horrible than pen can describe." But she was able to help some of them. Cordelia rescued a 14-year-old boy who had come south as a servant to one of the doctors. The doctor left him after he became ill. Cordelia had him sent back to his home in Adams County, Wisconsin. She wrote, "It was worth a year's hard labor to see the joy of the little fellow."

Kids in the Civil War

It was not unusual for Cordelia to meet teenage soldiers. Around 76,000 young boys under 18 years old are known to have served in Civil War armies. The actual number may have been even higher. Many young boys lied about their age so that they could join the army.

Many boys began their life in the army as musicians. Each company in an **infantry** regiment had a drummer. This boy would play drum beats to awaken the soldiers in the morning and to signal lights out at night. Drums were used on the battlefield to send orders from the officers to

WISCONSIN VETERANS MUSEUM 98-1-529

WISCONSIN VETERANS MUSEUM 64-131

the soldiers. The drumbeats told them where to go. Drummers often played along with a fife, which is a high-pitched instrument similar to a flute.

Cavalry regiments did not use drums and fifes. Instead, they used bugles to sound the different calls in camp and on the march. There are many stories of buglers who were too small to climb

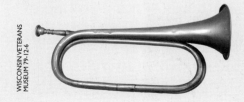

WISCONSIN VETERANS MUSEUM 79-12-6

onto their horses without help. Some of these young musicians later traded their instruments for guns and fought.

infantry (**in** fuhn tree): the part of an army that fights on foot

Johnny Clem was perhaps the most famous young boy to fight in the Civil War. He was born in Ohio, and he ran away from home at age 9 to become a Union drummer boy. He tried to **enlist** when he was 10 years old, but he was turned away because he was so young and so small. This didn't stop Johnny. He tagged along with some soldiers from Michigan. After a while, they let him be their drummer and fight along with them. Johnny fought in the Battle of **Chickamauga** at the age of 12. In that battle, he shot a Confederate colonel who had warned him to surrender. Johnny was promoted to sergeant for his bravery. He'd become the youngest volunteer soldier ever to become an officer in the United States Army.

Johnny Clem was the most famous boy soldier in the Civil War.

Can you imagine how brave a boy had to be to play music while bullets and shells were exploding all around him? Would you have been brave enough to do that?

---

enlist: join the military   **Chickamauga**: chik uh **maw** guh

47

WHI IMAGE ID 75360

Although Cordelia reported to Governor Salomon that she was tired at night, she wrote, "In the morning I am quite rested & ready again for my labor. Surely my God & Father has watchful care over me."

Cordelia loved her job. She wrote that she was "grateful to the Governor every day for the position in which he has placed me." She worked hard and promised to work harder. Her confidence continued to grow. In a letter to the governor, she wrote:

> You do not imagine how much I have to do & how well I do it.... Do not fear to ask me to do any thing because you fear it is difficult or unpleasant. If I can do it, I am glad to.

Cordelia's good work continued to be noticed by others. In December 1862, the *Memphis Bulletin* printed a letter from Colonel Allen. He wrote that he had seen Cordelia work in camps and hospitals in Memphis and Helena, towns in Tennessee. "She is a true **patriot**," he wrote. "She has the courage to volunteer to help in dangerous places near where there are battles. She has the good heart to take care of the wounded. She gives hope to the sick and comforts the dying." He finished with these words: "What the best, highest, and wisest can do, she is **accomplishing**."

Cordelia was not afraid to deal with difficult problems. In January 1863, she wrote that during her visit to a hospital in Ironton, Missouri, she saw a doctor who was often drunk when he treated the soldiers. She also found a **steward** who starved soldiers from the 11th Wisconsin Regiment. She gathered **evidence** from officers and people living in Ironton. Both the doctor and the steward were fired from their jobs because of the evidence Cordelia provided.

A sergeant from the 11th Wisconsin Regiment. Cordelia visited this regiment in 1863.

patriot: a person who loves his or her country   accomplishing: succeeding at doing   steward: an officer in charge of providing food for soldiers   evidence: information and facts that help prove something really happened

Cordelia also had a new suggestion for Governor Salomon. The more time she spent working in the southern hospitals, the more convinced she became that the soldiers would have a better chance of getting well if they were moved to hospitals in the North. In the warm southern air, wounded soldiers lay in dirty, unhealthy rooms where **infection** and disease spread quickly in the heat and **foul** air. The poor **ventilation** caused many problems.

Cordelia believed that many of the diseases spread because of the "bad air." She recommended opening special state military hospitals in Wisconsin to treat soldiers suffering from wounds and diseases. She believed that the healthy air of Wisconsin would help them recover more quickly. The soldiers agreed. They told her, "If only we could breathe the Wisconsin air, we could get well. We could get our strength." What's more, the extra care the patients would receive from family and friends in Wisconsin also would help them to recover. In the months ahead, Cordelia would become even more convinced of her idea to send the soldiers north.

infection: an illness caused by germs or viruses   foul: rotten   ventilation (ven tuh **lay** shuhn): system that allows fresh air into a room and sends stale air out

There was one major **obstacle** to the plan. When the Civil War began, sick and wounded soldiers could usually return to their homes to recover. The army changed this rule in 1863. Now soldiers were kept in military hospitals to recover. Many of these hospitals were located in the South. Some governors in the North, including Governor Salomon, wanted to have army hospitals built in their own states. President Lincoln did not want this to happen. He was afraid that the soldiers would **desert** once they recovered.

Bad Air: PU!

When something smells bad, kids often say, "PU!" "PU" is short for *puteo,* which is the Latin word for "to stink."

At the time of the Civil War, doctors knew little about what caused disease, how to stop it from spreading, or how to cure it. Many people thought diseases were caused by "bad air" or *miasmas,* the Greek word for "pollution." Of course, bad air in hospitals often contained many germs. But it wasn't until after the Civil War had ended that scientists like **Louis Pasteur** discovered that many diseases were caused by germs instead of bad air.

---

obstacle (**ob** stuh kuhl): something that prevents another thing from happening   **desert** (di **zurt**): run away from the military   **puteo**: poo **tay** oh   **miasmas**: mɪ **az** muhs *or* mee **az** muhs   **Louis Pasteur**: **loo** ee   pa **stur**

It made sense for people during the Civil War to think that the air might be causing diseases because the smells were so bad. Soldiers were supposed to bathe once a week, but they often ignored this. They often had no changes of clothing, and so their clothes were dirty and smelled bad, too. It was said that you could smell a Civil War army on the march before you could see it.

The Civil War hospitals smelled especially bad. Ventilation was poor, so bad smells remained in the air. Smells from toilets and from the dead bodies of soldiers were common. Smells of rotting flesh from wounds that were not healing filled the air. Water was often in short supply at hospitals, so clothes, bedding, and the soldiers themselves were rarely washed.

Almost every letter Cordelia sent to Governor Salomon included comments about the "miasmas" in the crowded hospitals. She didn't write about how much these smells bothered her. She wrote that the bad air was making the soldiers sick.

When Cordelia herself became so sick that she had to return to the North, she thought her sickness was caused by a miasma. When she recovered in the North, she believed that it was the healthy northern air that led to her recovery.

Although Cordelia was wrong that it was "bad air" that made her sick, she was correct that she and the soldiers were more likely to recover in the North. The northern hospitals were less crowded and cleaner than the southern hospitals. The food was healthier, and there was more of it. The soldiers' families helped to take care of them. This made the northern hospitals better places for sick and wounded soldiers.

By 1863, many of Wisconsin's soldiers had heard of Cordelia and the things she did to help soldiers. In January, she was helping men in a St. Louis hospital. That's when she heard that there were many sick and wounded soldiers in Memphis, too. These men asked that Cordelia come to visit them. Cordelia immediately went to Memphis.

Sergeant Edwin Eason from Columbus, Wisconsin, was one of the soldiers who asked for Cordelia. She hurried to see him, but he died before she reached him. His last words were, "Send for Mrs. Harvey & she will help me home." Even as he was dying, the sergeant trusted that Cordelia would take care of his final wish to be sent home to be buried.

Traveling between hospitals was often difficult for Cordelia. She described having to walk a half mile "in the meanest mud I ever saw" on her trip to visit a hospital in Rolla, Missouri.

Sometimes it was dangerous for Cordelia to go from one hospital to another. Once she traveled on a **steamer** that was protected by a **gunboat**. The gunboat fired its cannons into the woods along the river because the soldiers on board heard that Confederate soldiers were attacking boats on the river. Cordelia was not a bit afraid.

LIBRARY OF CONGRESS PRINTS AND PHOTOGRAPHS

Cordelia traveled on a gunboat like this one.

steamer: a large boat powered by steam   **gunboat:** a small ship armed with guns

In March of 1863, Cordelia traveled to Vicksburg, Mississippi. General **Ulysses** S. Grant was there leading the Union army in a battle to capture the Southern city of Vicksburg. Cordelia met with General Grant to suggest how he could help the wounded soldiers.

WHI IMAGE ID 9517

Ulysses S. Grant was the general in charge of the Union army.

General Grant agreed to make all of the changes Cordelia suggested. He agreed that there should be a medical inspector in every regiment. Medical inspectors would have the power to discharge men unfit for service. He also promised to work to make the hospitals cleaner. General Grant would become the president of the United States 3 years after the war ended.

Cordelia soon returned to Memphis. She looked for soldiers who were so weak that they would never be able to fight in the war again. When she found them, she had doctors examine them. They often were discharged and sent home. Cordelia saved many lives this way.

Ulysses: yoo **lis** eez

She continued to ask Governor Salomon to open a military hospital in Wisconsin. The warmer weather was particularly difficult for soldiers stuck in the crowded, poorly ventilated hospitals. Many sick and dying soldiers from Wisconsin begged Cordelia, "Can't we go home?"

In less than a year, she would meet with Abraham Lincoln to try to convince him to build hospitals in the North closer to soldiers' homes.

7

"Dead Men Cannot Fight"

In April 1863, Cordelia became too sick to continue her work as a sanitary agent. She returned to Madison briefly and then went to New York to recover. She knew that she could stay with her family who lived there. Cordelia realized that being close to family would help her to recover. She felt better after only a few months. Her return to health convinced her even more that many soldiers would get better just as she had by receiving treatment in the North, breathing good air, and being closer to family.

Cordelia returned to Madison in August 1863. She was now so popular that the *Wisconsin Daily State Journal* wrote about

city. Of course every body in town will see it before they sleep to night.

MRS. HARVEY.—This lady, the widow of the late lamented Governor HARVEY, arrived in this city on Saturday afternoon. She is in good health. She has rendered much valuable aid to the Wisconsin sick and wounded soldiers during the past year. Many a heart has been made glad through her kind ministrations, and her many friends will rejoice to learn of her entire recovery from sickness contracted during her benevolent and patriotic mission—doing good to the afflicted soldiers.

PERSONAL.—We are happy to learn that Capt. THEODORE READ son of Prof. READ,

The *Wisconsin Daily State Journal* welcomed Cordelia back home.

her homecoming. They reported that Cordelia was healthy again from the sickness she caught while "patriotically caring for Wisconsin's soldiers."

Cordelia soon met with Governor Salomon. Together, they decided to try to change President Lincoln's mind about the military hospitals. They drew up a **petition** asking that hospitals for soldiers be opened in Wisconsin. They **circulated** copies of the petition, and 8,000 Wisconsin citizens signed them. In September 1863,

Many people from Wisconsin signed the petition asking President Lincoln for a hospital to be built in the state.

petition (puh **ti** shuhn): a letter signed by many people asking those in power to change a law or rule
circulated: sent around

Cordelia Visits Washington, D.C.

Madison

Mississippi River

Ohio River

Washington, D.C.

AMELIA JANES, EARTH ILLUSTRATED, INC.

Cordelia visited President Lincoln at the U.S. capital.

Cordelia brought the petitions to Washington, D.C. There, she planned to meet President Lincoln face-to-face.

Cordelia was not nervous about meeting the president. She knew that she was arguing for a cause that was important to Wisconsin and to the rest of the country. Military hospitals in the North would help Wisconsin's fighting men. Good northern hospitals would make the Union army stronger by helping soldiers fully recover.

When Cordelia arrived in Washington, she went straight to the White House. In her hands was a letter from a Wisconsin senator explaining why she had come. Immediately, she was led into the president's office.

In a speech she gave after the Civil War, she described her meeting with the president in great detail. When she entered his office, she found the president reading. She described him as "tall and lean, and he sat in a folded up sort of way in a deep arm chair."

President Lincoln raised his eyes, asking, "Mrs. Harvey?" She replied, "Yes, I am glad to see you, Mr. Lincoln."

He took her hand and said he hoped she was well. But Cordelia reported that she saw "no smile of welcome on his face." Instead, "he had the **stern** look of a judge who had already decided against her."

Abraham Lincoln in 1863, the year Cordelia visited him.

stern: serious

60

Cordelia could tell from his look that he did not want to open the hospitals.

President Lincoln said, "Madam, this matter of northern hospitals has been talked of a great deal, and I thought it was **settled**, but it seems not. What have you to say about it?"

Cordelia replied, "Only this, Mr. Lincoln, that many soldiers in our army on the Mississippi River must have northern air or die. There are thousands of graves all along our southern rivers and in the swamps for which the government is responsible."

Cordelia then argued that many more men would be made well if they were sent to northern hospitals than if they stayed in the South.

Lincoln said, "Yes, yes, I understand you; but if they are sent north, they will desert; where is the difference?"

"Dead men cannot fight," Cordelia answered, "and they may not desert." President Lincoln said angrily, "They would desert."

settled: decided

Even though she was speaking with the president, Cordelia had to disagree. She replied, "You must pardon me when I say you are mistaken; you do not understand our people. . . . They are true and loyal to the government."

After a moment Lincoln spoke again. "Well, well, Mrs. Harvey, you go and see the **secretary of war** and talk with him and hear what he has to say." He picked up the letter Cordelia had given him, and after writing something on the back of it, handed it to her.

After Cordelia left President Lincoln's office, she read what he had written. It was a short note to Secretary of War Edwin Stanton. It said, "**Admit** Mrs. Harvey at once; listen to what she says; she is a lady of intelligence and talks sense." It was signed "A. Lincoln."

Cordelia immediately went to see Secretary Stanton. After she explained what she wanted, Stanton said he had sent the

---

secretary of war: person who reports directly to the president to give advice about war and to carry out the president's decisions   **admit**: let in

surgeon-general to New Orleans to examine all the hospitals. Nothing could be done until the surgeon-general returned.

What Stanton told her wasn't entirely true. Stanton was **stalling** because he didn't want there to be northern hospitals. Like President Lincoln, he believed soldiers would desert from the army after they recovered. Cordelia returned to President Lincoln and told him about her conversation with Stanton. She ended by saying, "I have nowhere else to go but to you."

President Lincoln knew that Secretary Stanton did not want to give in to Cordelia. He said that he would speak with Stanton himself and asked Cordelia to return the next morning. Cordelia got up to leave, but President Lincoln told her not to hurry away. Cordelia wrote that he "spoke kindly of my work, said he fully appreciated the spirit in which I came. He smiled pleasantly and **bade** me good evening."

As Cordelia left the White House, she saw a **congressman** she knew. She told him about meeting with President Lincoln.

He asked, "How long are you going to stay here?"

surgeon-general: the chief of medical services in the army or navy   **stalling**: delaying doing something on purpose
bade (bayd): told or said   **congressman**: a member of Congress, where laws are decided for the United States

"Until I get what I came after," she replied.

When Cordelia returned to the White House the next morning, she could tell that the president was in a bad mood. He waited for her to speak, but she didn't. Finally, he asked, "Have you nothing to say?"

"Nothing, Mr. President, until I hear your decision. Have you decided?"

"No, but I believe this idea of northern hospitals is a great **humbug**, and I am tired of hearing about it."

Cordelia replied that she did not want to add any more problems to the many he already had. "I would rather have stayed at home," she said.

With a kind of half smile, he said, "I wish you had."

But Cordelia was there for a cause she believed in. She said, "I came to **plead** for the lives of those who were the first to **hasten** to the support of this government, who helped to

---

humbug: bother   **plead**: to ask with great emotion   **hasten** (**hay** suhn): move quickly

64

place you where you are, because they trusted you. . . . I know that a **majority** of them would live and be strong men again if they could be sent north. I say I know, because when I was sick among them last spring, surrounded by every comfort, with the best of care, and **determined** to get well, I grew weaker day by day, until my friends brought me north. I recovered entirely, simply by breathing northern air."

Lincoln snapped, "You **assume** to know more than I do."

Cordelia's feelings were so hurt that she almost cried. Instead, she said: "You must pardon me, Mr. President . . . it is because I *do* know what you do not know, that I come to you. . . . I believe the people have not trusted you for **naught**. The question only is whether you believe me or not. If you believe me you will give me hospitals."

The president said, "You assume to know more than surgeons do."

---

majority: more than half of a group of people or things
assume: suppose something is true without checking it
determined (di **tur** mind): committed to work hard at
naught (nawt): nothing

To this Cordelia replied, "Oh no, Mr. Lincoln, I could not perform an amputation nearly as well as some of them do." She reminded him that she had spent many months visiting soldiers, often from early morning to night. "I come to you from the cots of men who have died," she said, "who might have lived had you permitted."

Then she gave one last appeal. "[The soldiers of Wisconsin] have been faithful to the government. . . . They will be loyal to the government. . . . If you will grant my petition you will be glad as long as you live."

Cordelia began to feel like she was taking up too much of the president's time. She rose to leave and asked if he had made a decision about her request.

He replied, "No. Come tomorrow morning at 12 o'clock."

8

"You Are Perfectly Lovely to Me, Now, Mr. Lincoln"

The next morning Cordelia woke up with the feeling that she had failed. She was sure that the president would say no.

When she returned to the White House, she had to wait 3 hours before the president came into the room where she was waiting. This was the first time she had seen him standing. She wrote, "He was very tall and moved with a **shuffling**, awkward motion."

He came forward rubbing his hands saying, "My dear Madam, I am very sorry to have kept you waiting."

The president sat down in a chair next to Cordelia. He had good news. He had ordered a hospital for soldiers in Wisconsin.

shuffling: walking slowly, hardly raising your feet

Cordelia could not speak. She was so surprised by this decision that she cried for joy. Then she said, "God bless you. I thank you in the name of thousands who will bless you." The president asked Cordelia to return the next day. He promised to give her a copy of the order to open the hospital.

When Cordelia returned to the White House the next morning, she found more than 50 people in the waiting room. Cordelia gave her name to wait her turn, but she did not have to wait. She was led right into President Lincoln's office. He smiled and said, "Come here and sit down." He gave her the copy of the order.

President Lincoln told her that he would name the hospital after her. Cordelia asked him to instead name it after her husband, Louis. He agreed to do this. He said he had admired Governor Harvey and was sad that he had died.

Cordelia thanked President Lincoln. She said he'd been very kind to her.

The president looked at Cordelia with a smile and asked her if she thought he was handsome. Cordelia answered,

"You are perfectly lovely to me, now, Mr. Lincoln." This made the president laugh.

When Cordelia rose to leave, she said simply, "God bless you, Abraham Lincoln." Soon after Cordelia returned to Madison, she received a letter from Secretary Stanton. He wrote that he had ordered the opening of the Harvey United States Army General Hospital in Madison.

It did not take long for the hospital to open its doors. The Harvey Hospital opened in October 1863 with 106 patients. It was located on the east side of Madison in a large home that used to belong to a Wisconsin governor.

This octagon-shaped house near Lake Monona became the Harvey Hospital. It was once a governor's home.

WHI IMAGE ID 37423

69

Two other military hospitals would later be opened in the state, one in Milwaukee and one in **Prairie du Chien**.

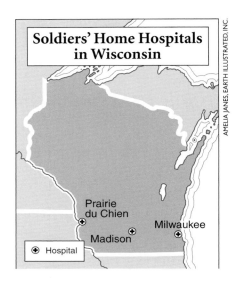

Soldiers' Home Hospitals in Wisconsin

AMELIA JANES, EARTH ILLUSTRATED, INC.

Prairie du Chien
Milwaukee
Madison
⊕ Hospital

As Cordelia expected, the soldiers promised to fight even harder when they recovered from their injuries. In a letter to the *Wisconsin State Journal* on January 2, 1864, one group of soldiers wrote:

> We had a superb dinner yesterday.... It did both body and soul good. It makes us feel happy to realize that we have friends at home, it makes us more patriotic.... Each of us inwardly **determines** that he will fight better, when returned to the [battle] field, to defend a Government under which **reside** so many noble women.
>
> Truly yours,
> The Soldiers of Harvey Hospital

Prairie du Chien: prair ee doo **sheen**   **determines**: decides   **reside** (riz **id**): live

70

By "noble women" they meant Cordelia, the Wisconsin Angel who made the Harvey Hospital possible. The hospital stayed open until the summer of 1865, shortly after the Civil War ended. It had been home to more than 600 men.

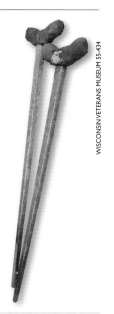

WISCONSIN VETERANS MUSEUM 55-434

This pair of crutches was used at Harvey Hospital by Almeron Willis Stillwell.

The Father of the Wisconsin Dells

Henry Hamilton (H.H.) Bennett was one of the most famous patients at the Harvey Hospital. In 1861, Henry joined the 12th Wisconsin Regiment. He served 3 years as a private and fought in several battles. In 1864, he was wounded in his right hand when he accidentally shot himself with his own gun. He was sent to the Harvey Hospital to recover and stayed for several months.

WHI IMAGE ID 66547

H.H. Bennett in uniform.

71

Henry had worked as a carpenter before the Civil War, but his injury made it impossible to work with both hands. So, the following year, he bought a photography business in his hometown of Kilbourn, Wisconsin. Later, Kilbourn became Wisconsin Dells. Henry became famous for his invention of a stop-action shutter in 1888. This invention allowed him to take photographs of events as they were happening. Before the stop-action shutter, people had to sit still for a photograph, often for several minutes. If they moved, the picture would be blurry.

Henry also became well known for his photographs of the caves and rocks of the Wisconsin Dells and the surrounding area. His photographs made the Dells a world-famous place to visit. Because he helped make the Wisconsin Dells become so popular, Henry is sometimes called "the Father of the Dells."

WHI IMAGE ID 2101

H.H. Bennett's most famous photograph was taken in the Wisconsin Dells.

9

"We Knew You Would Come"

Cordelia did not stay in Madison to help with the Harvey Hospital. Instead, she returned to Memphis, Tennessee, in October 1863 to continue her work as a sanitary agent. In early November, she received a letter from Governor Salomon asking her to go to Vicksburg, Mississippi, to help Wisconsin soldiers in the area. In Vicksburg, Cordelia reported that so many soldiers on both sides of the war had been killed that "when one hears how and sees where they have suffered, the wonder is not that so many died, but that any lived."

A Civil War soldier ready for battle.

The Battle of Vicksburg

Vicksburg, Mississippi, was an especially important city during the Civil War. It was located on the banks of the Mississippi River. President Lincoln and General Grant were convinced that the key to winning the war was to gain control of Vicksburg.

At the beginning of the war, the Confederate army controlled Vicksburg. That meant they controlled the soldiers and supplies that traveled down the Mississippi. If the Union army took control of the city, they would be able to send Union soldiers and supplies anywhere on the Mississippi River.

By 1862, General Grant had control of the entire river, except for 200 miles below Vicksburg. In May 1863, he marched his

The city of Vicksburg during the battle. Can you see the Union tents near the Mississippi River at the top of this photograph?

74

soldiers about 25 miles south of Vicksburg. They crossed through swamps and **bayous** along a very difficult route. No one thought an army could pass through these swamps, but they made it.

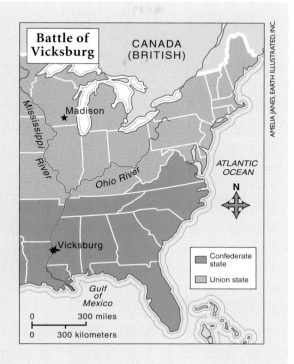

The Union army soon surrounded Vicksburg. They created a **blockade** so that food and supplies could not get to the people in the city. For 2 months, no food or supplies went in or out of Vicksburg. Grant's plan was to starve the city into surrendering. Cannons also **shelled** the city for 48 days.

Grant's plan worked. There was so little food in Vicksburg that people there were forced to eat rats, cats, and dogs. On July 4, 1863, the Confederate army at Vicksburg surrendered. This was one of the most important Union victories during the Civil War. It also left behind great destruction, many deaths, and many starving people.

bayou (bī oo): a stream that runs through a swamp, leading to a lake or river   **blockade**: an area that is closed off so that people and supplies cannot go in or out   **shelled**: bombed with a canon

75

Cordelia soon came upon a problem. Some soldiers from Wisconsin were in jail. They had been there for several weeks. She visited them and learned that they were not guilty of any crimes. She spoke with the authorities and arranged for these innocent men to be freed. Some had bravely fought in the Battle of Vicksburg earlier that year.

Cordelia also met a soldier who was in jail for refusing to **reenlist**. He did not want to stay in the army.

She reminded him of the duty he owed to his country. She convinced him to reenlist. He thanked her for helping him to understand that he should be patriotic. The prisoner might have stayed in jail for a long time without Cordelia's help. Instead, he returned to his regiment and promised to "cheerfully perform [his] duty as a soldier."

In March 1864, Cordelia brought a new shipment of food for soldiers from Wisconsin. She described how important it was for them to receive such supplies from their home state. "It was enough to break one's heart to see the sick &

reenlist (ree en **list**): rejoin the army after completing a first term of service worn out," she wrote. "Poor fellows, they lay in the dust, dirty, ragged & no appetite & if they had [an appetite], [they had] nothing to eat but **hardtack** & bacon, which lay piled up in one corner of the tent in the dirt."

Worms for Breakfast, Lunch, and Dinner!

Soldiers have always complained about their food, but Civil War soldiers had a lot to complain about. A poor diet was one of the main causes of sickness and disease during the war.

Soldiers usually ate the same thing each day. Their main food was a crackerlike biscuit called "hardtack." Hardtack was so hard that it had to be soaked in a liquid like water or coffee to make it soft enough to chew. Sometimes hardtack was filled with worms. Soldiers then called the hardtack "worm castles." Many soldiers ate the hardtack at night so that they wouldn't have to see the worms while they ate them.

Many soldiers ate rotten food and got sick. Refrigerators had not yet been invented. There was no safe way to store food, so

hardtack: a biscuit similar to a cracker

it often spoiled. Soldiers also got sick because they didn't cook their food long enough. Eating undercooked food made them sick.

Soldiers sometimes had little to eat for several days. When the food wagons arrived, they stuffed themselves. Going back and forth between not eating at all and then eating too much was not good for their health. They often received food **rations** for several days all at once. Hungry soldiers would often eat 3 days of food in one day. Then they wouldn't eat anything the following 2 days. When they were training or marching, many soldiers would faint from weakness because they hadn't eaten for several days.

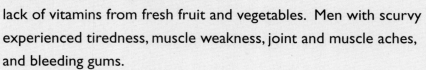

Often, the only kind of food that soldiers ate was not what their bodies needed. They rarely had fresh vegetables or fruit to eat. During the Civil War, many soldiers got a disease called scurvy. Scurvy comes from a lack of vitamins from fresh fruit and vegetables. Men with scurvy experienced tiredness, muscle weakness, joint and muscle aches, and bleeding gums.

As the war went on, the food got worse and worse. This was partly because it was hard to get food to the soldiers. Often there was enough food, but it was not where the soldiers were.

ration (**rash** uhn): a limited amount, especially of food

This was especially true when the armies were on the march because their supply wagons couldn't keep up with them. Sometimes dishonest people sold rotten food to the soldiers, too.

Food sent from home was one way soldiers got better things to eat. For the sick and wounded, food given out by the sanitary agents might be the only way they received healthy food. One reason that sick and wounded soldiers looked forward to Cordelia's visits was that she brought them good food to eat.

Cordelia asked one young soldier if there was anything special he'd like to eat. He said, "If I could have some green **stewed** apples, they would taste good."

Cordelia asked, "Baked apples?"

"No! No. *Stewed* apples," he replied.

Cordelia hurried to get supplies for the soldiers, including stewed apples for the young boy. The soldiers had not expected Cordelia to return. She came just in time for supper. She shook out their blankets, and brought

stewed: cooked for a long time over low heat

the soldiers water so that they could wash their hands and faces. While they were changing into the clean clothes she had brought them, she put out plates of beef, bread and butter, and apples for them to eat. The soldiers couldn't believe how lucky they were to have such good food for supper. They said, "Oh, how good this is."

Cordelia wrote Governor Salomon to tell the women from Wisconsin how happy they'd made the soldiers by sending them tasty food: "I would not exchange the memory of their grateful faces, & their heartfelt 'God bless you's' for any thing in this world. Tell our people the good they have done, but also tell them not to '**weary** doing.' I could fill volumes like this, but I have no time to write it—nor you to read it. Believe that I am doing all that I can do."

In April 1864, Cordelia visited a river boat in Vicksburg that had suffered heavy losses while carrying slaves to freedom.

weary (**wee** ree): get tired of doing

She found the deck covered with dead and wounded slaves and soldiers. Many of the slaves had been freed from plantations.

One of the doctors recognized Cordelia and said, "Mrs. Harvey, come away! You can do nothing. These men have had no care since they were wounded. . . . They will be put in hospitals here and cared for as soon as possible." Cordelia asked if they had any supplies and was told, "Nothing! Nothing!" One of the nurses said, "Oh, Mrs. Harvey, [please] bring us some sponges & small **syringes** to dress wounds and some lint too!" Cordelia hurried away and soon returned with the supplies they needed.

Cordelia asked the doctor in charge of the boat for permission to come on board and go to work. He thanked her and invited her to help. Many of the soldiers were from Wisconsin. They recognized Cordelia and said, "We knew you would come."

syringe (suh **rinj**): a medical instrument used to clean wounds

81

Sometimes Cordelia took care of soldiers even when there were reports of dangerous diseases nearby. In June, she wrote, "It is very warm and we have been having a great deal of rain. Some fear **yellow fever**, and say there have been several cases in New Orleans brought on a Mexican **vessel**. I have no **dread** of it for myself."

In October 1864, Cordelia received a wonderful surprise. The 2nd Wisconsin Cavalry gave Cordelia a present to thank her for her loving care. Captain Ring, an officer from Milwaukee, made a presentation to Cordelia on behalf of all

the soldiers in his regiment. He gave her a beautiful watch and chain. This unexpected gift touched Cordelia's heart. She felt **honored** that the soldiers would thank her for what she called "the little that I have done."

Soldiers gave this watch and chain to a surgeon who had cared for them. Cordelia received a similar gift.

yellow fever: a disease passed on to humans through the bite of a mosquito   **vessel**: a boat or ship
dread: fear   **honored** (on urd): given praise, made to feel special

As the war continued, conditions in the hospitals slowly got better for the soldiers. The hospitals and camps were cleaner. More supplies became available, and they also reached the hospitals sooner.

During one of her hospital visits, Cordelia saw a boy named Charley whom she'd visited in the same hospital 6 months earlier. He'd been so weak she thought he would die. She made sure he stayed in the hospital for several weeks until he was strong again. Then he returned to his regiment. He soon got sick again, however. When Cordelia visited, he had been back in the hospital for 5 months.

Cordelia told Charley he needed a discharge or at least to go home to recover. But Charley said, "No." He had promised to serve in the Union army, and he wanted to keep his promise. He said that if he was too weak to fight, he could still help in other ways. Cordelia wrote, "Oh was I proud that he was a Wisconsin boy. This kind of boy is not **confined** to Wisconsin however. The country is full of them."

confined: only found in

Cordelia became sick once again in November. She continued working as best she could. She refused to be paid when she could not work.

By now, the Wisconsin soldiers knew where Cordelia could be found in Vicksburg. They would contact her if they were in a hospital in the area and needed her help. She might go to their hospital to help them or write a letter to the hospital authorities to help the soldiers.

As the war drew to a close in 1865, Cordelia began working with the Southern prisoners who were in hospitals. She gave them food, clothing, and kind words, just as she had the Union soldiers.

Cordelia now reported to Wisconsin's new governor, James Lewis. She would send him lists of which soldiers from Wisconsin had died and which soldiers were still prisoners. Many families back in Wisconsin often did not know what had happened to the men they had sent to the war. Cordelia's reports helped the governor let families learn news of their husbands, sons, and fathers.

Andersonville:
The Worst Civil War Prison

Cordelia saw many Union soldiers who had been prisoners in Sumter County, Georgia, near the village of Andersonville. Andersonville Prison was known for its overcrowding, **starvation**, disease, and **cruelty**.

Andersonville was perhaps the worst military prison of the entire Civil War. The prison had no buildings at all. The only shelter came from tree branches, bits of wood, and whatever blankets soldiers had with them when they were captured. The soldiers used these materials to build tents and **lean-tos**. In summer, soldiers had nothing to protect them from the scorching sun.

The conditions at Andersonville Prison were terrible.

starvation: to suffer or die from lack of food   **cruelty**: behavior that causes great pain or suffering   **lean-to**: a shack or shed supported on one side by trees or posts

LET US FORGIVE. BUT NOT FORGET.

Why do you think this drawing of Andersonville has this title?

Many developed terrible blisters. Some became totally blind. In the winter, some froze to death. Andersonville had no doctors or hospitals for the sick or wounded.

Andersonville was always crowded. Diseases spread quickly among the prisoners because they lived so close together. There were many other problems that also caused prisoners to die. Many prisoners starved to death or became sick and weak because of the lack of food. There wasn't enough food, and the only food they had was poor. A prisoner might have only a few tablespoons of beans or peas a day. There wasn't enough water, either. The water came from Sweetwater Creek, but it was anything but sweet. In fact, the prisoners had to drink from the same creek in which they washed and dumped the contents of their **privies**.

Ole Hanson was a Wisconsin soldier who was in prison at Andersonville.

From February 1864 to April 1865, over 45,000 Union soldiers were prisoners at Andersonville. Of these, almost 13,000 died from disease, poor sanitation, **malnutrition**, overcrowding, and lack of protection from the weather. At one point, an average of more than 100 prisoners died there every day.

When Cordelia met men who had survived Andersonville Prison, she wrote to Governor Lewis: "[If you] could hear them relate the horrors through which they have passed, you would wonder that a man was left to tell the tale. Many are entirely broken in health and spirits, but generally they are improving rapidly.... Oh, how we love to do for them, they have suffered so much."

Aren't you glad that you weren't a prisoner at Andersonville Prison?

privy (**pri** vee): an outdoor toilet; an outhouse   **malnutrition**: a harmful condition caused by not having enough food or by not eating healthy food   **Ole**: **oh** lee

87

10

A Home for Hundreds of Children

Besides caring for soldiers, Cordelia also worried about children whose fathers had died during the war. Who would take care of these children?

Sometimes, the mothers couldn't take care of their children. Before the war, women usually stayed home to

The sewing machine, invented in 1844, made it easier for women to earn money as seamstresses.

cook, clean, and care for their children. Men earned money to support their families. When the men died, many families were left without any income. Some women found work as **seamstresses** and **domestic servants**, but many more had no money, no job, and no idea how to support themselves and their children.

seamstress: a woman who sews for a living   **domestic servant**: a paid housekeeper

Day care centers did not exist at that time. Women couldn't take care of their children and work at jobs to earn money at the same time.

If children had no relatives or friends who could take care of them, they were sometimes sent to **poorhouses**. Many of the poorhouses were very dirty and unhealthy. They were terrible places for children.

Some children with no one to care for them were sent to local jails. The jails were perhaps the worst places for children. They had to live there with adults who were **criminals**.

In the 1850s before the Civil War, religious organizations had opened several orphans' **asylums** in Wisconsin. The asylums were located near Milwaukee and took care of small numbers of children. But in 1865, the loss of more than 11,000 Wisconsin soldiers in the Civil War meant the entire state of Wisconsin had a much bigger problem. Now, there were more than 6,000 **orphans** in Wisconsin.

poorhouse: a place where people were sent when they didn't have enough money to take care of themselves
criminal: someone who commits a crime   **asylum** (uh sı luhm): a place for people to live who cannot live on their own   **orphan**: a child whose parents have died

Early in 1865 while she was in Vicksburg, Cordelia wrote a letter to Governor Lewis. In it, she asked him to open an **orphanage** in Wisconsin. She argued that almost every other state already had an orphanage for the children of "our fallen heroes."

When she returned to Madison in the summer of 1865 after the Civil War had ended, Cordelia brought 6 orphans with her. She never asked whether their fathers fought for the North or the South. When she learned that the government was going to close its army hospitals in Wisconsin, she thought that the Harvey Hospital could be turned into a home for soldiers' orphans. She began working to make it happen.

Cordelia quickly raised the necessary money for the orphans' home. She convinced the government and people who owned businesses to help her. On January 1, 1866, only 6 months after the Harvey Hospital had closed, the building was reopened as the Soldiers' Orphans Home for the State of Wisconsin. Cordelia was chosen to be the superintendent.

orphanage (or fuhn idj): a place where children who have no parents live and are looked after

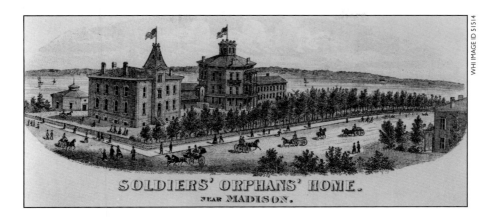

WHI IMAGE ID 51514

SOLDIERS' ORPHANS' HOME.
NEAR MADISON.

By the time the Orphans Home opened, Cordelia had many
more requests for orphans to live there than there was room.
She decided to allow 84 orphans to move into the Orphans
Home immediately. The children were 3 to 13 years old. Most
of these children arrived with only the clothes they were
wearing. Cordelia ordered extra clothing right away.

What was the day like for children in the Orphans Home?
During the day, the children went to the school in the
orphanage. They studied reading, spelling, geography, math,
grammar, and writing. There were signs on the classroom
walls reminding them that they would not be forgotten by the
people of Wisconsin, even though they had no fathers.

The orphans and staff pose in front of the Wisconsin Soldiers' Orphans Home in 1870, 5 years after the end of the war.

Lucius Fairchild lost his left arm in the war.

Each child was also required to do chores. The boys cut wood, hauled coal, milked cows, fed hogs, took care of gardens, and fixed shoes. The girls helped with the cooking and sewing.

Visitors often came to the Orphans Home. Lucius Fairchild was a war hero who became governor. He had taken good care of the men who served under him. Now that the war was over, he'd sometimes take the children out for picnics on Sundays.

92

He spent every Christmas Eve with them. To him they were "the little children of our fallen **comrades**."

How did the children feel about the home? Coming to Madison must have been hard for most of them. Many had lost their fathers in the war. Many had mothers who couldn't take care of them. All of them had been sent away from their homes and friends to live with a large group of strangers. Some had never gone to school before. Now they sat inside a schoolroom for most of the day.

The children also must have felt confused about their place in the world. As soldiers' orphans, they were "different" from other children. Many people felt sorry for them. Many people also felt that their fathers were heroes and that the children were special.

After one and a half years as superintendent, Cordelia decided her work was finished. More than 300 children had lived in the Orphans Home by then. She knew each of their names. The Orphans Home remained open until 1874.

comrade (**kahm** rad): a companion in war

A total of 683 children lived there from 1866 to 1874. Cordelia had begun working in the Civil War helping Wisconsin's soldiers. Her work ended by helping their children.

Wisconsin Soldiers' Orphans Home Remembered

In 1908, students in the public schools of Madison were asked to give up to 5 cents for a **memorial** marker for the Harvey Hospital. The marker still stands today more than 100 years later near the location of the hospital. The memorial honors both Cordelia and Louis Harvey. It reads:

> On this city block, during the Civil War, stood Harvey Hospital, and later the Wisconsin Soldiers' Orphans Home, both **established** through the influence of Mrs. Harvey, whose honored husband, Governor L. P. Harvey, had accidentally been drowned in the Tennessee River, at Pittsburg Landing, Tenn. near the Shiloh battlefield, April 19, 1862, where he had gone after the battle, with supplies for the comfort of the sick and wounded Wisconsin soldiers.

memorial: something that is built or done to help people to continue to remember a person, place, or event
established: started

After Cordelia left the Soldiers' Orphans Home in May 1867, she returned to Shopiere. Nine years later, she married Reverend Albert Chester. Reverend Chester had been the pastor of a **Presbyterian** church for many years. After they married, they lived in Buffalo, New York. There Albert was the principal of the Buffalo Female Academy, a school for girls. Cordelia's younger sister, Irene, taught

Cordelia's second husband, Albert T. Chester.

drawing and painting there. Cordelia became a teacher again, too. It had been more than 30 years since she'd taught at the Southport Academy. When Albert died in 1892, Cordelia returned to Wisconsin.

Presbyterian: prez buh **tir** ee uhn

95

Once back in the state, Cordelia taught Sunday school at a church in Fort Atkinson. Some of her students remembered her as "a little woman with a sweet face hidden under a small bonnet with a long widow's veil; a loving personality, quick, **keen** and jolly."

Cordelia died in the home of her sister, Ellen, in Clinton, Wisconsin, on February 27, 1895, at the age of 70. She was buried in Madison's Forest Hill Cemetery next to Governor Harvey.

In her letters to Wisconsin's governors, Cordelia did not brag about her work. Instead, she often wrote about "the little that I have done" to help the soldiers. Looking back at her life, it is clear that she did much more than a little to help the soldiers and the children of Wisconsin. It's easy to understand why people called her the Wisconsin Angel.

keen: sharp-witted

Appendix

Cordelia's Time Line

1820 — Louis Harvey is born in East Haddam, Connecticut, on July 22.

1824 — Cordelia Perrine Harvey is born in Barre Center, New York, on December 7.

1840 — Cordelia moves with her family to Southport (now Kenosha), Wisconsin.

1841 — Louis moves to Southport, Wisconsin. He becomes the principal and a teacher at the Southport Academy.

1841 — Cordelia becomes a teacher at the Southport Academy.

1847 — Cordelia and Louis are married. They move to Clinton Junction, Wisconsin, and open a general store.

1847 — Louis is elected to the Wisconsin Constitutional Convention.

1848 — Mary Harvey, daughter of Cordelia and Louis, is born.

1851 — Cordelia, Louis, and Mary move to Waterloo, Wisconsin. Louis opens a flour mill.

1852 — Mary Harvey dies from scarlet fever.

1859 — Louis is elected secretary of state of Wisconsin. He and Cordelia move to Madison.

1861 — Louis is elected governor of Wisconsin.

1862 — Louis drowns in the Tennessee River on April 19.

1862 — Cordelia becomes Wisconsin's sanitary agent.

1862–1863 — Cordelia visits hospitals along the Mississippi River to see how Wisconsin soldiers are treated.

1863 — Cordelia meets with President Lincoln and convinces him to establish military hospitals in Wisconsin.

1863 — The Harvey Hospital opens in Madison, Wisconsin.

1865 — The Civil War ends, and the Harvey Hospital is converted into the Soldier's Orphans Home for the State of Wisconsin.

1865 — The Soldiers' Orphans home opens on January 1. Cordelia becomes its first superintendent.

1876 — Cordelia marries Reverend Albert T. Chester. They move to Buffalo, New York.

1892 — Reverend Albert T. Chester dies. Cordelia returns to Wisconsin.

1895 — Cordelia dies on February 27 at the age of 70.

Glossary

Pronunciation Key

a	cat (kat), plaid (plad), half (haf)		**oh**	open (**oh** puhn), sew (soh)
			oi	boil (boil), boy (boi)
ah	father (**fah** THur), heart (hahrt)		**oo**	pool (pool), move (moov), shoe (shoo)
air	carry (**kair** ee), bear (bair), where (whair)		**or**	order (**or** dur), more (mor)
			ou	house (hous), now (nou)
aw	all (awl), law (law), bought (bawt)		**u**	good (gud), should (shud)
ay	say (say), break (brayk), vein (vayn)		**uh**	cup (kuhp), flood (fluhd), button (**buht** uhn)
e	bet (bet), says (sez), deaf (def)		**ur**	burn (burn), pearl (purl), bird (burd)
ee	bee (bee), team (teem), fear (feer)		**yoo**	use (yooz), few (fyoo), view (vyoo)
i	bit (bit), women (**wim** uhn), build (bild)		**hw**	what (hwuht), when (hwen)
I	ice (Is), lie (lI), sky (skI)		**TH**	that (THat), breathe (breeTH)
o	hot (hot), watch (wotch)		**zh**	measure (**mezh** ur), garage (guh **razh**)

99

abolished (uh **bol** ishd): officially ended

accomplishing: succeeding at doing

adjutant-general (**aj** uh tuhnt **jen** ruhl): the highest-ranking officer in the army after the governor

admit: let in

aid society: a group that is formed to help others

allotment commissioner (kuh **mish** uh nur): person whose job it was to decide how much of soldiers' pay should be sent to their families

amputated: cut off of the body because of disease or injury

army camp: a place where an army stays in tents or other temporary homes

assume: suppose something is true without checking it

asylum (uh **sı** luhm): a place for people to live who cannot live on their own

attractive: pretty or handsome or pleasant to look at

awkwardly: clumsily, without skill

bade (bayd): told or said

battlefield: an area where a battle is being fought

bayou (**bı** oo): a stream that runs through a swamp, leading to a lake or river

best-informed: having the most knowledge or information

bid: tell or say

blockade: an area that is closed off so that people and supplies cannot go in or out

capital: the city where the state government is located

cavalry (**ka** vuhl ree): soldiers who fight on horseback

Civil War: the war between the North and South of the United States, which took place between 1861 and 1865

circulated: sent around

coat of arms: a design in the shape of a shield that is used as the special sign of a family or city

company: a unit of 50 to 100 soldiers

comrade (**kahm** rad): a companion in war

congressman: a member of congress, where laws are decided for the United States

Confederate (kuhn **fed** ur it): related to the group of 11 Southern states who fought the Northern states during the Civil War

confined: only found in

constitutional (kon stuh **too** shuhn uhl) **convention**: a meeting where state leaders write down what rights and responsibilities people of the state will have and how the government will work

consumption: a highly contagious disease that usually affects the lungs, also known as tuberculosis

contagious (kuhn **tay** jis): catching, able to be spread by close contact

cot: an army bed

Crimean (krɪ **mee** uhn) **War**: a war between Russia and Turkey, Great Britain, France, and Sardinia fought from 1853 to 1856

criminal: someone who commits a crime

cruelty: behavior that causes great pain or suffering

desert (di **zurt**): run away from the military

determined (di **tur** mind): committed to work hard at

determines: decides

discharged: officially told to leave the military

discipline (**dis** uh plin): control over the way you act or behave

domestic servant: a paid housekeeper

dread: fear

drill: learning through repeating the same action over and over

duty: something someone is required to do

dysentery (**dis** uhn tair ee): a contagious disease with symptoms of fever, diarrhea, and stomach pain

enlist: join the military

equal: able to handle

established: started

evidence: information and facts that help prove something really happened

exposed: put in contact with a contagious disease

foul: rotten

frustrated: feeling helpless and discouraged

general store: a store that sells a variety of items such as clothing and tools

geography (jee **og** ruh fee): the study of the earth, including its people, resources, climate, and physical features

governor: the person elected as the head of the state to represent all of the people of the state

gratitude: a feeling of being thankful

gunboat: a small ship armed with guns

hardtack: a biscuit similar to a cracker

hasten (**hay** suhn): move quickly

honored (**on** urd): given praise, made to feel special

humbug: bother

impulse: a sudden thought or idea that leads someone to take action or do something

income: the amount of money someone earns or receives regularly

infantry (**in** fuhn tree): the part of an army that fights on foot

infection: an illness caused by germs or viruses

inflamed: swollen

inspire: influence or encourage someone to do something

keen: sharp-witted

labor: work

lean-to: a shack or shed supported on one side by trees or posts

legislature (**lej** uh slay chur): a group of people elected by citizens who have the power to make the laws for the state

lieutenant (loo **ten** uhnt) **governor**: the second in command to the governor

limestone: a hard rock used in building and in making cement

103

lint: small bits of thread or fluff used like a bandage for covering wounds

majority: more than half of a group of people or things

malnutrition: a harmful condition caused by not having enough food or by not eating nutritious food

medical inspector: the person who makes medical arrangements for a unit of the army

memorial: something that is built or done to help people continue to remember a person, place, or event

mourning (**mor** ning): feeling sadness or grief for someone who has died

naught (nawt): nothing

obstacle (**ob** stuh kuhl): something that prevents another thing from happening

orphan: a child whose parents have died

orphanage (**or** fuhn idj): a place where children who have no parents live and are looked after

patriot: a person who loves their country

persuaded: convinced someone to do something by giving the person good reasons

peninsula (puh **nin** suh luh): a piece of land that sticks out from a another land mass and is almost completely surrounded by water

petition (puh **ti** shuhn): a letter signed by many people asking those in power to change a law or rule

plain: simple or not fancy

plantation: a large farm

plead: to ask with great emotion

pneumonia (nuh **mohn** yuh): a disease that causes the lungs to be filled with fluid, making breathing difficult

politics: the way a city, county, state, or nation governs itself

poorhouse: a place where people were sent when they didn't have enough money to take care of themselves

privy (**pri** vee): an outdoor toilet; an outhouse

prospect: something that is looked forward to

pull-away: a game similar to tag

quartermaster: an officer in charge of providing housing, clothing, food, fuel, and transportation for soldiers

ration (**rash** uhn): a limited amount, especially of food

recovering: getting better after illness or injury

reenlist (ree en **list**): rejoin the army after completing a first term of service

regiment (**rej** uh muhnt): a unit of 500 to 1,000 soldiers

reputation (rep you **tay** shuhn): the opinion that people have about someone or something

reside (riz **id**): live

sanitary (**sa** nuh tair ree): having to do with being clean and healthy

scarlet fever: a serious and quickly spreading illness that occurs mostly in children, and causes a bright red rash, a sore throat, and a high fever

schoolmistress: a woman who teaches in a school

seamstress: a woman who sews for a living

seceded (si **see** ded): left or withdrew from a group or an organization, often to form another

secretary of state: the person elected as keeper of the official records of the government of a particular state

secretary of war: person who reports directly to the president to give advice about war and to carry out the president's decisions

settled: decided

shelled: bombed with a canon

shuffling: walking slowly, hardly raising your feet

stalling: delaying doing something on purpose

starvation: to suffer or die from lack of food

state senator: a member of the state senate, the group that determines the laws of the state

steamer: a large boat powered by steam

stern: serious

steward: an officer in charge of providing food for soldiers

stewed: cooked for a long time over low heat

superintendent (soo pur in **ten** dent): the person in charge of an organization

surgeon (**sur** juhn): a doctor who performs surgery

surgeon-general: the chief of medical services in the army or navy

syringe (suh **rinj**): a medical instrument used to clean wounds

telegram: a message that is sent by telegraph

tuberculosis (tuh bur kyuh **loh** suhs): a highly contagious disease that affects the lungs, and often leads to death

typhoid (**tı** foid): a contagious, often deadly disease with symptoms of high fever and diarrhea

unfit: unable to serve because of illness or injury

Union (**yoo** nyuhn): the group of states that remained loyal to the United States government during the Civil War; the North

ventilation (ven tuh **lay** shuhn): system that allows fresh air into a room and sends stale air out

vessel: a boat or ship

wages: the money someone is paid for his or her work

ward: a large room or section in a hospital where patients are taken care of

ward master: the person in charge of a hospital ward

weary (**wee** ree): get tired of doing

yellow fever: a disease passed on to humans through the bite of a mosquito

Zouave (zoo **ahv** *or* zwahv): the name of several volunteer regiments in the Civil War

Reading Group Guide and Activities

Discussion Questions

- After her husband's death, Cordelia chose to take up some of Louis's work in caring for Wisconsin soldiers. Why do you think she chose this path? How do you think it helped her?

- Cordelia lived during a time when many women did not have the chance to do important work outside of the home. Why was being chosen a sanitary agent so important to her? In what ways did such a position help her to grow?

- When Cordelia spoke with President Lincoln, she insisted that soldiers from Wisconsin were "patriotic" and "loyal." Why did she choose these 2 qualities to make her argument to the president?

- When people praised her work, Cordelia said she was "simply doing my duty & doing very little compared with the great amount there is to be done." Why do you think she downplayed her role? What did she mean by "the great amount there is to be done"?

- In what ways was Cordelia's idea about helping Civil War orphans similar to helping soldiers? In what ways was it different?

Activities

- Visit your local historical society or museum and draw or take pictures of items from the Civil War, such as bullets, cookware, or medical supplies. Write a report telling what you learned about each item and who you think might have used it.

- Pretend you are a Civil War nurse and write 5 diary entries of your experience working at the newly opened Harvey Hospital or at one of the hospitals Cordelia visited in the South.

- With your class, write a short play from one of the scenes in the book. Assign a director, actors for each part, costume designers, and prop makers. Add details to make the story more realistic. Describe what you want the costume designers and prop makers to create.

- Enlarge a map of the United States to create a poster-sized map of Cordelia's journeys. Add labels and pictures to show what happened at each location.

To Learn More about the Civil War

Chang, Ina. *A Separate Battle: Women and the Civil War*. New York: Puffin, 1996.

Herbert, Janis. *The Civil War for Kids: A History with 21 Activities*. Chicago: Chicago Review, 1999.

Malone, Bobbie, and Kori Oberle. *Wisconsin: Our State, Our Story*. Madison: Wisconsin Historical Society, 2008.

McPherson, James M. *Fields of Fury: The American Civil War*. New York: Atheneum for Young Readers, 2002.

Murphy, Jim. *The Boys' War: Confederate and Union Soldiers Talk about the Civil War*. New York: Clarion, 1990.

Pferdehirt, Julia. *Caroline Quarlls and the Underground Railroad*. Madison: Wisconsin Historical Society, 2008.

Stanchak, John E. *Eyewitness: Civil War*. New York: Dorling Kindersley, 2000.

Stotts, Stuart. *Lucius Fairchild: Civil War Hero*. Madison: Wisconsin Historical Society, 2011.

Wroble, Lisa A. *Kids During the American Civil War*. New York: PowerKids, 1997.

Acknowledgments

As a boy, I loved to read biographies about Abraham Lincoln. In one of my favorite stories, Abe happily worked for 3 days to pay for a book he had damaged. He loved reading and books so much that he was thrilled to actually be able to own one, even if it meant working hard to help a farmer harvest his corn to earn the money. Only now as an adult do I realize that I connected with this story because I shared his love for reading and for books.

When Bobbie Malone, director of the Office of School Services at the Wisconsin Historical Society, asked me to consider writing a book about Cordelia Harvey, I accepted without ever imagining that Abe Lincoln would figure so prominently in the enterprise. I also never imagined that Cordelia would be one of the most compassionate and competent people I've ever encountered. Thank you, Bobbie, for sending me on this delightful journey that allowed me to explore the inspiring life of Cordelia Harvey, reconnect with Abe Lincoln, and learn about so many different facets of the Civil War.

I am fortunate to have friends and family members who read the early drafts of this book and made many suggestions that improved this telling of Cordelia's story. Thank you to Caroline Hoffman, Shayle Kann, Judy Landsman, and Deborah Waxman for your invaluable feedback. I am also grateful to Sara Phillips and Bobbie Malone, both intrepid editors at the Wisconsin Historical Society Press, for helping to shape this book and adding much valuable historical background to the story. Thanks also to Andrew White and Diane Drexler of the Wisconsin Historical Society Press for their apt image and production work.

Index

This index points you to the pages where you can read about persons, places, and ideas. If you do not find the word you are looking for, try to think of another word that means about the same thing.

When you see a page number in **bold** it means there is a picture on that page.

Harvey Zouaves, 15

Henry IV of France, 3

Hibbard, Mary, 3

Hibbard Perrine, Irene, 95

hospitals, *See* military hospitals

Howe, Timothy, 22, 23, **23**

I

illness, *See* disease

instruments, *See* musical instruments

Ironton, Missouri, 37, 49

J

Jackson, Lieutenant General Thomas "Stonewall," 16

jails, 76, 89. *See also* prisoners

K

Kenosha, Wisconsin, 4, **4**, 5

Kilbourn, Wisconsin, *See* Wisconsin Dells, Wisconsin

L

ladies aid societies, *See* aid societies

Lewis, James, 84

Lincoln, President Abraham, 2, 10, 51, 56, **60**, 63, **65**

    meetings with Cordelia, 60–62, 64–66, 67–69

M

Madison, Wisconsin, 9, **9**, 57

    Forest Hill Cemetery, 96

    Ladies Aid Society, 17

Manassas, Virgina, 16

maps,

    Civil War battles, **11**, **75**

    Missouri, **29**

    Northeastern U.S., **59**

    Wisconsin, **6**, **70**

marriage of Cordelia, 6

measles, 31

medical inspectors, 41, 55

Memphis Bulletin, 48

Memphis, Tennessee, 39, 53, 55, 73

military hospitals, 35, 37, **41**

  case for opening in the North, 50-51, 56, 57, 58-59, 61-66

  conditions in, 30, 52-53, 83

  in Wisconsin, 67-71, 90

  See also Harvey Hospital

military ranks, 40

Mississippi River, 35, 74

Mound City, Illinois, 18

musical instruments, 46

N

New York, 57

nicknames, 2, 35, 42

Nightingale, Florence, 42, 43-44, **43**

nurses, 27-28, 36, 43-44, 81

  soldiers as, 30-31

  See also sanitary agent, Cordelia as

See also Union Ladies

O

orphanages, 89-91, **91**, 92-94, **92**

orphans, 88-94

P

Paducah, Kentucky, 18

Pasteur, Louis, 51

Perrine, John, 3

petition, 58, **58**

photography, 72

Pittsburg Landing, **19**

plantations, 10

pneumonia, 37

poorhouses, 89

praise for Cordelia, 38, 48-49

prisoners, 37-38, 84, 85-87

Q

Quiner, Emilie, 27-28

R

ranks, *See* military ranks

Republican Party, 10

Ring, Captain George W., 82

Rock County, Wisconsin, 8

Rolla, Missouri, 54

S

Salomon, Governor Edward, 22, 25, **25**, 38, 58, 80

sanitary agent, Cordelia as, 25–26, 33, 48–51, 53–56, 73, 76–77, 84

visits with soldiers and, 29–32, 35, 37–42, 45, 55, 76, 79–82, 83–84

Savannah, Tennessee, 18

Sawyer, Nathaniel, 20

scarlet fever, 6

schooling, cost of, 6

scurvy, 78

secretary of state, Wisconsin, 8

secretary of war, 62

Shopiere, Wisconsin, 7, 95

sickness, *See* disease

slavery, 10

soldiers, 13–15, **13**, 24, 34, 70

children as, 45, 46–47

Confederate, 37–38, 84

diet, 77–78, 86–87

discharging, 35, 37, 41–42, 55

families of, 17, 53, 84, 88–90, *See also* orphans

Governor Harvey and, 14–15, 18

imprisoned, 76, 85–87

training of, 13–14

women as, 24

See also disease

See also military hospitals

Soldiers' Orphans Home for the State of Wisconsin, *See* Wisconsin Soldiers' Orphans Home

Southport, *See* Kenosha, Wisconsin

Wisconsin Dells, Wisconsin, 72, **72**

Wisconsin Soldiers' Orphans
Home, 90–94, **92**

women, 37, 88–89

as soldiers, 24

war efforts and, 16–17, **16**, 24,
34, 80

See also Union ladies

Y

yellow fever, 82

Z

Zouaves, 15, **15**